DON'T TELL GOD
I'VE LOST
FAITH!!

Faith; tested, lost, renewed!!

—— Book One of a Three Book Series ——

They are not lost who find
The light of sun and stars and God!!

THOMAS A. DORNFRIED

WESTBOW
PRESS®
A DIVISION OF THOMAS NELSON
& ZONDERVAN

Scripture taken from the King James Version of the Bible.

WestBow Press books may be ordered through booksellers or by contacting:

WestBow Press
A Division of Thomas Nelson & Zondervan
1663 Liberty Drive
Bloomington, IN 47403
www.westbowpress.com
1 (866) 928-1240

ISBN: 978-1-9736-8627-9 (sc)
ISBN: 978-1-5127-4580-1 (e)

Print information available on the last page.

WestBow Press rev. date: 02/11/2020

CHAPTER 1

HEART AND SOUL!

Dedication!!
Heart and Soul!!

"My mother passed away in April 1997
My father in May 2007"
The passing of my parents, burdened my very heart
I knew there was a reason, why they had to depart
I know in my heart, they're in a better place
But try telling that, to my doubting face
Tried to wonder why, God took them from me
Read His Word and prayed, are the answers I received
These poems that I write, from the very start
Are spoken from the heart, with words from the soul!

DEDICATION!!

"In memory of my loving mother Virginia,
Who was my Heart
Who never once lost faith in me
And my caring father Alfred
Who was my soul
It is from him that I have the strength to carry on!!

Years have passed!!
Hebrews 11:1

NOW FAITH is the substance of things hoped for,
The evidence of things not seen

The years have passed
All the tears have dried
When she passed away
That's when I cried

Then there are the days
I recall in my mind
Of much better days
Of those precious times

I wish that I had
That of another day
To speak from my heart
Words I wanted to say

Now my mother's home
In skies that are blue
To my sweet mother
"I sorely miss you!!"

Our Dad!!
Psalm 18:32

It is God that girded me with strength, and makes
My way perfect

Our Dad loved us from the very start
With a warm and tender caring heart,
You could tell by his calloused hands
Of the hard life he led as a Man

Though he was rough, deep leathered skin
He always showed gentleness, from within,
Though our Dad is no longer in this place
We can still feel his heart filled embrace

Though he is gone, to whom we miss
We will remember his oh so gentle kiss,
He is finally Home, where he truly belongs
With our Mother, singing praises in song!!

From the heart!!

These words that I write
From the depths of my Soul
To tell all of the World
Life is not always cold

Yes, there are trials
Some large, some small
Some cause you to stumble
Others cause you to fall

Yet through of all of these
There is a chance of hope
That when you're at your end
Don't let go of the rope

I write these words
Straight from the heart
So let these words
From you, never part!!

To my dad!!

To my father, my dad
Though you are not here
To this, I'm truly sad

In words, you did not teach
But by your example
Is the goal I shall reach

You taught me to be strong
To face all tribulations
What ever comes along

You taught wrong from right
To stand for myself
Never give up; **FIGHT!!**

CHAPTER 2

SIGHT, UNSEEN!!

Walking by Faith!!

SIGHT UNSEEN!!

We walk by faith sight unseen
Each and every day
Hoping to on the narrow path
Trying not to stray

It is God in whom we should trust
With our all
Trusting He will always be there
When you fall

To walk by faith is not easy
No, no indeed
To have complete faith in God
Is what you need

It takes tons of courage; strength
To walk each day
It takes tons of courage; strength
Daily to pray

Pray to God each day to have faith
This you should do
Then complete faith you shall receive
Oh this is true!!

Mini Inspirational Poems

M I P #1

Faith is much more than just a word
A way of life it should always be
You should have faith everyday
Not just in the times of need!!

There will be mountains in your life
Which come in shapes and sizes?
It takes the faith of a mustard seed
To all mountains in your life!!

Why have faith!!

Oh why have faith
Oh why indeed
Is it something I want?
Is it something I need?

Do I need it now?
Do I need it today?
Will it help my life?
Will it help in anyway?

I've lived this long
I've lived alone
When I am away
When I am at home

From help, I need none
From help, let me be
Without faith, I can breath
Without faith, I can see

In my life, I need no guide
In my life, I need no lead
So why should I have faith
So why oh why indeed!!

M I P #2

Everyday is a journey in our lives
Times we don't know where to go,
So when you feel all turned around
Your path to you, God will show!!

Sometimes we no not lie ahead
Sometimes we no not the future
Sometimes we no not what's in store
All the time, God will always be there!!

Faith's Foundation!!

You can say your faith is strong
To the very point of pride
You can say that oh so loud
But what do you keep inside

You can tell the whole World
From the very mountain top
But when your faith is tested
To the World do you stop?

You can tell to all you see
Your is faith is oh so strong
But when trials come your way
Does you faith stay that long

When tests of faith, come your way
On what foundation will it stand?
Will it stand on solid ground?
Or that of sinking sand!!

Facing Tomorrow!!

How do you face tomorrow?
Let alone today
When lacking the courage
To simply find a way

I don't about you
But as for me
When facing the unknown
I simply want to flee

I lack the courage
To face the unknown
I just want to hide
Just simply stay at home

This is called being human
Oh yes, oh yes indeed
Not to ask for help
In daily what we need

But I have found the courage
No longer I'm in sorrow
It's in my faith in God
That helps face tomorrow!!

Mustard Seed!!

A mustard seed is tiny
Is not very big
A mustard seed is tiny
Is no larger than a fig

This tiny mustard seed
Moves Mountains so big
This tiny mustard seed
No larger than a fig

How can this tiny seed
That is so very small
How can this tiny seed
Do it all

It has so much faith
It what it can do?
It has so much faith
You should too

To move Life's Mountains
Here's what you need
To move Life's Mountains
Is faith that of a mustard seed!!

M I P #3

We don't know what's ahead
Around the corner; things we dread
When you don't know what to do
"Amazing Grace" will see you through

We walk our lives each day
By most, by any means
We walk our lives by faith
With God, who's unseen!!

Facing Giants!!

We all face giants, at home, work or school
If not conquered, our lives they will rule

When facing giants, we run away, we hide
Feeling oh so helpless, very deep inside

We lack the courage, to face them on our own
We just stand there, frightened, so all alone

When facing giants, we tremble at our knees
We can not move, we just simply freeze

There is a weapon, our giants we can face
It is God, giving courage, giving grace

God is on our side; to us He is truly cares
Ask Him for help, do this just by prayer

If you want to conquer giants, there is a way
It is faith in God, in giants you can slay!!

Faith!!
(Where's yours??)

We walk by faith, each and everyday
Not realizing, someone guides our way
Earthy possessions, we put our faith and trust
Sooner or later, all of these turn to dust

Putting our faith in gold, is that what we need?
Riches in Heaven, is where our faith should be
Our fellow man, should we have faith in this?
Not putting faith in God, is the goal we shouldn't miss

Putting faith in ourselves, is another story
There are times; we seek our fame and glory
With all these things, we gladly put faith in
With all these things, we'll loose; never win

So take a leap of faith that is completely blind
It will you loosen you up, helping you to unwind
It's our faith in God, we need to completely trust
We may loose faith in Him, but in Him not in us!!

What is faith??

What is faith, is it real
It is trust, that's the deal

Faith is love, helps you cope
When you need, gives you hope

Where's your faith, is it here
Do you know, do you care

It's in God, faiths in you
Yes it is, yes it's true

Why have faith, why at all
It will help, when you fall

With no faith, you will find
You'd be lost, all the time

Is your faith, day by day?
Is your faith, here to stay??

CHAPTER 3

DON'T TELL GOD!!

Faith, Lost!!

Before the fall!!

Before the fall
I had it all,
Faith as deep as the Sea
Then when I fell
I could not tell,
What just happened to me?

Life was easy
Oh so breezy,
This feeling would not last
What was before
Was soon no more
It was now in the past

Before the fall
I had it all,
My faith moved mountains big
Then when I fell
Soon I could tell
My faith could not move figs

No longer easy
Not so breezy,
I felt as this could last
What was before
Is now no more,
I wish for this to past!!

THE WATCH!!

My eyes lid up, the watch I did see
Hoping it would be a present to me

It had a fifty-seven Chevy inside
The year I was born it did coincide

Powder blue was the color of the car
Admired close up in the window jar

I told my Mother, told my Dad
Getting this watch will make me glad

Received the watch before my birthday
Began to cry, tears of joy got in the way

My mom passed way, it was time to go
This watch is bittersweet, this I know

The reason this watch is close indeed
It was the last gift my Mom gave me!!

Saying "Goodbye"

The time had come, oh so near
The time had come, that I feared

It had to come, this I know
It had to come, oh is woe

The phone call came, it was night
The phone call came, filled with fright

There was my mom, in the bed
There was my mom, this I dread

No longer in pain, pain in chest
No longer in pain, peace and rest

There were tear drops, from my eyes
There were tear drops, saying "Goodbye!!

M I P #4

Your path will be filled with traps
Your path will be filled with snares
Your path will be filled with pitfalls
Your path will be filled with hope!!

The lowest point of your life is now
The lowest point of your life hits you hard
The lowest point of your life is rock bottom
The lowest point of your life; God lifts you up!!

In A Flash!!

In an instant, in a flash
I lost my faith
Just like that
It is gone, it was here
I'm not concerned
I don't care

In an instant, in a flash
God took my mom
Just like that
She is gone, she was here
I cried for her
Shedding tears

In an instant, in a flash
Angry at God
Just like that
Faith is gone, faith was here
I'm not concerned
I don't care!!

Don't tell God!!
(Pt 1)

Don't tell God I've lost faith
Please do not tell Him at all,
How did this happened to me
All I remember is the fall

One day I was doing so well
Life was good, all was right,
Then it hit me all at one time
The beginning of my plight

My faith was strong as could be
Nothing could bring me down,
I was on top of the World
Then I fell; hard towards the ground

Loosing my faith is a sickness
A cancer eating away at my soul,
Not only are the nights oh so long
They are also so dark and cold!!

M I P #5

Clouds of doubt; aches and pain
My heart can't bear the strain
A storm has come; wind and hail
Now my faith begins to fail!!

Getting discouraged, day by day
Getting discouraged, so many ways
Getting discouraged, it's not okay
Getting discourage, here to stay!!

Tomorrow never came!!

Thought I had plenty of time
To tell my mom, "I love you"
Thought I had tomorrow
I was wrong, this is true

There she lay, in her bed
Full of such good cheer
I was glad to see her
I was glad she was there

Then God took her away
My heart; filled with sorrow
Thought I had one more day
Thought I had tomorrow!!

Though She's Not Here!!

My Mother is with God
In her Heavenly Home
Though she's not here
I am never alone

She is in my life
She is in my heart
Her love for me
Shall never part

Her soft, tender voice
Her soft, tender kiss
To both of these
I surely do miss

Though she's been gone
These so many years
I feel her presence
As if she's still here

Though she's not here
I am never alone
For my Mother is with God
In her Heavenly Home!!

PRIDE!!

If you want peace of mind
In the path, you should follow
There's a difficult thing to do
It's you pride, you should swallow

Pride will rear its ugly head
Hit you where you stand
So be the better person
Be it woman, child or man

If you peace in your heart
To start this very day
Don't let human pride
To get in your way

You know that pride is wrong
Your heart, listen to its call
It will ease this bad feeling
For pride will make you fall!!

If possible!!

From your family
Would you hide?
Loss of faith
Kept inside

From the world
All your friends
Tell no one
Till the end

From God above
Faith you've lost
Till what point
At what cost

From yourself
Kept inside
Loss of faith
Would you hide!!

By A Thread!!

Hanging by a thread, it's a mess
Being held by, weight of stress
It's so thin, so very small
Should it break, then I'll fall

It's so tiny, this piece of string
Can barely hold, to any thing
It's so thin, this piece of strand
If I fall, how hard will I land?

This thread is swinging, side to side
Feelings of sorrow, so deep inside
So much heartache, so much pain
My heavy heart, can't bare the strain

Want to let go, let this thread break
Want to let go, for Heaven's sake
There is not much, to hold to
One more pain, then I am through

Is there hope, from this stress?
Is there hope, please say yes
Here I am, it's here I will stay
Hanging by a thread, day by day!!

Confused!!

You've gotten confused
Lost; turned around
No one can hear you
Not even a sound

It's not all the hard
To get confused in life
With all your troubles
Problems lot's of strife

You've done all you could
It all came down to fail
Now you're more confused
Sit down, cry and wail

All of us get confused
It's nothing new at all
When this does happened
We trip, and then we fall

So when you get confused
Lost and turned around
Look up towards Heaven
The answer to be found!!

CHAPTER 4

GIVING UP THE GHOST!!

Hope, lost!!

Giving up the Ghost!!
(pt. 1)

There are trials: tribulations of life
They can cause heartaches; strife

Come straight on: or from left field
To these we succumb; simply yield

Deep down causing sorrow; fears
Breaking to our knees; into tears

Loosing sight; in what matters most
Causing us; in giving up The Ghost!!

DON'T TELL GOD!!
(pt. 2)

Don't tell God I've lost faith
This time I lost hope
Is this what it feels like?
To be at end of rope

These feelings that I have
I do not like them at all
Is this what it feels like?
From God, having to fall

Didn't tell my wife at all
Locked up deep inside,
I'm a much closed up man,
So human, so full of pride

My heart aches so much,
It is an agonizing pain,
No bright, sunny days,
Just those: gloom, pouring rain!!

Shattered Pieces!!
(Life, unglued!!)

Shattered pieces of my life
Come crashing to the floor,
Thought I had it all together
Of that I'm no longer sure.

Life is fragile oh so precious
Why waste it all on me,
Don't know why this is happening
How can this be?

Shattered pieces once broken then
Glued once more,
Then little by little
Those fragile pieces fell on the floor.

I came oh so close
Mending pieces of my broken life,
Then despair reared its ugly head
Adding to all this strife

Standing was once a strong willed man:
Who loved all
What stands before you
Is a man who took a terrible fall!!

M I P #6

Oh so heavy, are these chains
I am bound, am restrained
Oh so heavy, are these chains
So much anguish, so much pain!!

Can not rest, can not eat
Can not rest, can not sleep
Need a break, oh yes I do
Need a break, this is true!!

INTO THE DARKNESS!!

Into the darkness, I did plunge
My path, unknown, unclear
In to the darkness, I did plunge
No Angel would come near

Filled with darkness, not of sin
This battle, I can not win
Filled with darkness, not of sin
In my Soul, so deep within

Tunnel of darkness, never ends
Darker than any night
Tunnel of darkness, never ends
There's no Holy Light!!

CHAINS!!

I am chained, I am bound
I am sitting, on the ground
So much weight, so much pain
I am bound, with heavy chains

With heavy chains, weighing tons
Can not walk, can not run
More I move, more the strain
Here I sit all this pain

All this pain, in my soul
Feels like ice, so very cold
All my muscles, they do ache
Have to sleep, can not wake

Can not wake, from this dream
Want to yell, want to scream
Is there someone to hear my cries?
Tears of fear, from my eyes

From my eyes, tears that sting
I am numb, can't feel a thing
Here I sit, on the ground
I am chained, I am bound!!

M I P #7

It is dark, dark as night
There's no chance of any light
It is dark, in my Soil
Oh so lonely, oh so cold!!

I am lost, can not be found
Am confused, turned around
I am lost, as can be
"Oh my Lord, set me free!"!!

The Miry Clay!!

I am stuck, in miry clay
I am stuck, here to stay

No where to go, where to run
No where to go, where's the Sun

There are clouds, this very day
There are clouds, they're here to stay

I am down, from my core
I am down, please no more

I need help, I am alone
I need help, here at home

God, please answer my prayers
God, please I know you care

I am stuck, this very day
I am stuck, in miry clay!!

Giving up the Ghost!!
(pt. 2)

Loosing faith; like sinking sand
There's no place; no place to stand

I am tired; oh so weak
I am tired; oh so meek

Was alone; as can be
Did my God; abandon me

I had faith; sometimes most
Here I am; giving up The Ghost!!

Trapped!!

In a corner, a corner deep
Here I lay, here I sleep
All by myself, all alone
In my bed, in my home

My pillow's wet, tear stains
So much sorrow, so much pain
No where to run; to race to
Feeling trapped, this is true

But here I lay, in my bed
So much fear, so much dread
Blankets on me, I am wrapped
In my heart, I am trapped

My heart is beating; beating fast
This bad feeling, please do pass
Where to turn, where to go
To all of this, I do not know!!

One more day!!

One more day; sadness, pain
One more day; darkness, rain

What to do, this one more day
What to do, what's there to say

Why today, of all my life
Why today, there is much strife

One more day; heartache, pain
One more day; sorrow, strain

What to do, try hard to cope
What to do, is there still hope

When today, light from above
When today, God's Light of Love!!

Tell Me!!

Please tell me, why I should care
Life is cruel, life's not fair

It's not fair, what's in my life
Filled with pain, filled with strife

So much strife, it's everywhere
Why bother, I don't care

I don't care, no, not one bit
All I do, is have a fit

A fit I have, want to cry
Should I care, tell me why??

WHY SHOULD I!!

Why get out of bed
Why should I even care?
Life is oh so cruel
Life is so unfair

I've given up all hope
Giving it up all the away
I've lost all my faith
I lost, this very day

At one point in my life
My faith was very strong
At one point of my life
Everything went oh so wrong

Tomorrow starts a new day
The Sun will also rise
So why get out of bed
Why should I even try!!

Through the eyes!!

The time had come
Here I sit, end of rope
My heart weighing heavy
Felt there was no hope

The night was dark
So were my heart and soul
For I had lost all faith
My life was very cold

On the way to Church
Then off to Caroling
Still darkness in my heart
To the point it began to sting

Here I am at the point
The very point of despair
Then that was when God
Had answered my prayer

The prayer He did answer
The prayer that came from me
Was in the very form
Of precious Angels three

Each Angel gave a hug
So sweet and oh so mild
Then I sat in my truck
So God through eyes of a child

Happiness and blessed joy
Filled my heart and soul
Felt the presence of God
No longer was I cold

My faith had returned
My life I began to care
I began to cry
Joy was in my tears!!

Pieces, torn!!

Is your heart in pieces, torn?
Are you weak and weary worn?
Is your heart in heavy, chest?
No longer can get, any rest

Are you troubled, oh so blue?
No longer know, what to do
Do you think no one cares?
There's no hope, anywhere

To all this, I will say
There is hope, there's a way
What it is, you might ask
Is it easy, is it a task?

On your knees, you should pray
Pray to God this very day
He will help with all of these
All you need is to ask Him please!!

CHAPTER 5

DAWN OF A NEW DAY!!

Faith renewed!!

FROM THE MIRY CLAY!!

No longer stuck, in miry clay
No longer stuck, I'm on my way

Now I can move, I can run
Now I can run, towards the Sun

The clouds are gone, this very day
The clouds are gone, no longer to stay

Love lifted me, from my core
Love lifted me, give me more

God rescued me, no longer alone
God rescued me, in my home

He heard my pleas, God answered prayers
He heard my pleas, God truly cares

No longer stuck, in miry clay
No longer stuck, I'm on my way!!

M I P #8

Though your days be dark
Though your days be dreary
A new day brings light
A new day brings hope

When you are stuck in miry clay
When there is no where to go
Faith will lift you out
Faith will lead the way

Through the pain!!

Through the pain
Through it all
I will not falter
I will not fall

Despite the aches
Despite the pain
I have so much to give
I have so much to gain

Throughout the night
Throughout the day
I will not falter
I will not sway

I've not lost faith
I've not lost hope
Each day I will live
Each day I will cope!!

If Not!!

If not for love
If not for grace
If not for hope
I would be lost

If not for strength
If not for courage
If not for hope
I would be afraid

If not for friends
If not for family
If not for hope
I would be alone

If not for mercy
If not for God
If not for hope
I would not be here!!

NO LONGER CHAINED!!
"I am set free!!"

There was a time
When I was bound
Now I'm free
Now I'm found

When at this time
I could not cope
Now there's help
Now there's hope

Then there were times
When I had fright
Now there's comfort
Now there's light

Then came the times
When I was cold
Now I'm strong
Now I'm bold

Now is the time
That's come to me
No longer chained
"I AM SET FREE!!"

Love lifted me!!

From the depths of my soul
From my broken spirit

Came along "Amazing Grace"
Came along tender mercy

From the depths of my heart
From all of the pain

Came along amazing love
Came along tender rest

Love lifted my darkened soul
Love mended my broken spirit

Love lifted my burdened heart
Love healed all of my pain!!

Lost and Found!!
(Faith renewed)

Lost my faith, lost my way
Oh so many days

I was lost, I was blind
My faith, could not find

Dark were nights, dark were days
When I lost my way

Where was God, where was He
Here I am, on my knees

Came a Light, came my way
No more darken days

I was chained, I was bound
My faith now is found!!

All is well!!

All is well
With my life,
Even though
There is strife

At one point
Things were bad,
I was blue
I was sad

All is well
In my heart,
A brand new day
A brand new start

At one point
I was cold,
Now all is well
With my Soul!!

Hang In There!!

Has your rope
Come to its end
Aches and pains
You can not mend

Life's got you down
It's getting rough
Don't get discouraged
It's time to get tough

Dark are your days
Dark are your nights
At tunnels end
There is a light

This light's from Heaven
Will brighten your days
Will guide you along
Helping to find your way

So do not fret
Please have no fears
Take in a deep breath
Just Hang In There!!

SMILE!

In this Big World
So turn this sad look,
Turn it upside down

It's not that difficult,
That difficult to do
Just thing of something,
That's funny to you

Start with a giggle,
See, that wasn't bad
Deep in your heart,
You're feeling glad

Now just a minute,
A glow is on your face
That frown you had,
Has now been erased

Though we may be,
On this World for awhile
Make someone's day;
Give them a smile!!

Dawn of a New Day!!

With the dawn of a new day
Brought that of great hope
Through trials of faith
That brought end of rope

Though despair came along
Its ugly head it did rear
Never was there panic
Never was there fear

With the dawn of a new day
Renewed faith it did bring
From the depths of my heart
Eternal hope it did spring

No matter what comes in life
No matter what comes your way
Never fear life's darkness
For light brings a new day!!

CHAPTER 6

BLESSED ASSURANCE!!

Through it All!!

Blessed Assurance!!

It's what you'll find
When life is cruel
When all seems lost
When all is done

It's not from man
For him to give
For him to loan
For him to sell

It is for all
For girl and boy
For woman; man
For evermore

It is from God
With all His Love
With all His Grace
With all His heart!!

Heavy is your Cross!!

Heavy is your Cross
Oh so hard to bear
Heavy is your Cross
Does any body care?

All of your troubles
Seem be at a loss
All of your troubles
Weigh upon your Cross

It is a heavy burden
That It weighs you down
It is a heavy burden
Is there help to be found?

Heavy is your Cross
Burdened is your chest
Heavy is your Cross
Is there any rest

All of your troubles
That weighs you down
All of your troubles
There is help to be found

With this heavy burden
Which is hard to bear?
With this heavy burden
It is God, who truly cares!!

Blessed Assurance!!

It's what you'll find
When life is cruel
When all seems lost
When all is done

It's not from man
For him to give
For him to loan
For him to sell

It is for all
For girl and boy
For woman; man
For evermore

It is from God
With all His Love
With all His Grace
With all His heart!!

M I P #9
(Gods' Promise)

Never to leave
Never to part
From your life
From your heart

When you stumble
When you fall
I'll be there
Through it all!!

Inspirations!!

Inspirations that I receive
Are as diverse as can be
When I know one is there
It hits straight right at me

Then there are inspirations
That comes from good or bad
When I'm feeling happy
When I'm feeling sad

Inspirations come from death
Others come from life
When there is peace
When there is strife

They hit me at work
They hit me at home
If there wasn't any inspirations
There wouldn't be any poems

Inspiration from a Childs smile,
Inspiration from a song
When words comes to me
Writing a poem doesn't take long

So find what inspires you
That helps through your day
You're certainly to be blessed
In a very special way!!

Be not afraid!!

Be not afraid
Have no fears
Throughout the day
Throughout the year

Be not afraid
What lies ahead?
What tomorrow brings
Have no dread

Be not afraid
Have no fright
Throughout the day
Throughout the night

Be not afraid
Have no fear
Throughout your life
Be of good cheer!!

Comfort and Rest!!

Take comfort, take rest
Burden is your chest
Take comfort, take ease
God will give you peace

From daybreak, from start
Heavy is your heart
From daybreak, till night
God will make things right

Take comfort from strain
With all of your pain
Take comfort from strife
God will ease your life

Heavy is your heart
Burden is your chest
He'll always be there
For comfort and rest!!

Gods' Love!!

It will never leave
Will never disappear
Never goes away
It is always there

It has no strings
Not a one at all
Ask nothing from Him
He'll answer your call

It will stand steadfast
Built on solid ground
Stands the test of time
Even on shaking ground

To you it will not judge
In life, all that you do
Is not there for spite
Yes, this is oh so true

God's love will be there
In times you can not cope
His love will comfort you
Always giving you hope!

His Arms!!

They will comfort you
At your time you need,
In your darkest hours
Yes they will indeed

They won't let you fall
Hold you very tight,
For you are precious
In His Holy sight

They will keep you safe
From every alarm,
Always protecting you
From every harm

They will lift you up
Never let you go,
Through all your life
This you should know

When life gets you down
No cause for alarm,
You are always safe
Safe in His Arms!!

Never To Part!!

Have no fears
Have no fright
God will be there
To make things right

In the dark
In the cold
God gives you strength
To make you bold

In the day
In the night
You will always
Be in his sight

In your life
In your heart
God will be there
Never to part!!

Portion of Strength!!

To get you by
To see you through
A portion of strength
Is given unto you

It is from God
It's from above
Given unto you
Given with love

When life is hard
When life is blue
This portion of strength
Will see you through

It's just enough
It's inside of you
Never to part
Oh so true

Through days of Sun
Through days of Rain
This portion of strength
Will ease your pain!!

Storms of Life!!

When storms of life come your way
Do not bend, do not sway,
No longer have the will to cope
Never loose faith, never loose hope

Clouds of doubt bring aches and pains
All the stress, all the strain,
Winds will blow, turn cold with hail
All's not lost, all's not fail

How long will this feeling last
It will end, it will pass,
Ground around you turned to sand
Take Gods' love, take God's hand.

There's someone who'll help you
If you want, if you choose,
Lifting you up from stress and strife
God is hope, God is life!

Through it all!!

In days of sadness
In days of sorrow
God gives you courage
In facing tomorrow

In days of sunshine
In days of rain
God gives you comfort
In easing your pain

In days of despair
In days of fright
God gives you strength
In winning the fight

In days of worries
In days of woe
God gives you hope
In this; **you should know!!**

CHAPTER 7

HOPE IS...!!

Restored!!

Hope is...

Hope is... a child's hug
It chases the blues away
Warms up a tired heart
Brightens up your day
Knowing that a loved one
Is always at your side
In toughest of times
Turns frown; smile wide

Hope is... a kind word
From stranger or friend
Who'll always be there?
Helping hands to lend
You think you're alone
No one seems to care
At the very last second
Comes, takes away fears

Hope is... **the very glue**
Broken pieces it mends
Knowing in your heart
God's there; thick and thin
Never loosing your faith
No matter good or bad
When a special hug
Turns sadness to glad!!

M I P #10

Hope is here, day by day
Hope is here, when you pray
Hope will never, leave your side
Hope is what, you have inside

If not for hope, I'd surely be lost
If not for hope, my life it would cost
If not for hope that truly helped me
If not for hope, I fear where I would be

No Matter What!!

No matter what
Comes your way
God will be there
Each and every day

No matter what
Comes in life
God will be there
Helping with strife

No matter what
To you; life will send
God will be there
Always as a friend!!

Give Hope!!

Give hope to one another
To your sister, to your brother
For your Mom, for your Dad
To the ones, who are sad

Do not keep hope inside
In your heart, do not hide
To all; hope do you spread
To the ones, in fear and dread

Spread hope into the street
To all those you may meet
If you see some one who's down
Give them hope; change their frown

If you're timid, if you're shy
Do not worry, do not cry
Pray for those who can not cope
Pray for those; give them hope!!

No Longer!!

No longer in life
The will to cope

No longer in life
The will to care

No longer in life
The will to hope

Please in your life
Have strength to cope

Please in your life
Have strength to care

Please in your life
Have strength to hope!!

Always Have Hope!!

In darkness; night
In sunshine; light
In turmoil; mess
In heartache; stress
Always have hope!!

In sad times; blue
In glad times; too
In hard times; strife
In good times; life
Always have hope!!

In turmoil; can't cope
In worries; you mope
In travels; unclear
In life; you fear
Always have hope!!

M I P #11

All seems hopeless, all seems lost
Feels like you've run out of rope,
Don't loose faith in God above
Please don't ever give up hope!

When bad things happened to you
You feel like you can't get a break
No matter how bad life does get
To you, God will never forsake!

Where is hope??

Where is hope, you ask, you say
There is hope, it is today
Where is hope, from God Above
There is hope, it's in His Love

Always have hope, this is so true
Remember there's hope, when times are blue
Always have hope, do not let go
Remember there's hope, for God says so

There will be hope, day out, day in
God gives hope, in life to win
There will be hope, to you I say
God gives hope, from day to day

Where is hope, where can it be?
There is hope, for you, for me
Where is hope, you wish to know
There is hope, in God, it's so!!

Take Flight!!

Set your troubled soul free,
Soar towards the sky
Cast all your cares,
Leave them behind

Do not look down,
Look straight up above
Flying with eagles,
Flying with doves

So close your eyes,
A deep breath to take
God will never leave,
Never leave nor forsake

.

Soar through the clouds,
Each one and all
God has your hand,
He won't let you fall

Now you are soaring,
Eagle wings so light
Now you are soaring,
Let your soul take flight!!

A Hug!!

A hug is what you need
If hope is what you seek
Filled with so much love
This hug's from God above

A hug is filled with Grace
Your troubles it will chase
In times you can not cope
A hug will give you hope

A hug that's from a child
Is so sweet, oh so mild
When you're feeling blue
This hug is there for you

There are times in your life
You can not handle strife
When all of this it does bug
That's when you need a hug!!

Throughout the Year!!

Throughout the days
Throughout the year
Be of good heart
Be of good cheer

Have no worries
Concerns or fears
Throughout the days
Throughout the year

Throughout the days
Throughout the year
Be of strong faith
Be of strong cheer

Never loose hope
Along with cheer
Throughout the days
Throughout the year!!

Hope restored!!

There was a time, long ago
Filled with so much hope
I could handle, what came in life
Had no worries, I could cope

Then in an instant; in a flash
Hope disappeared; it was lost
Dark were my days, my nights
Aches and pains, my soul it cost

Thought there was, no more light
No longer would I care, at rope's end
Then in an instant, in a flash
Hope was restored, with my friends

Friends you see are children from Church
Giving me joy, giving me love
It was then that I knew
They were Angels from above.

When you think all is lost
In life no longer can you cope?
There's always is a chance
To have restored, life and hope!!

CHAPTER 8

THIS IS ME!! THIS IS YOU!!

Hanging tough!!

Imagine!!

A World without pain
No stress, no strain
No worries, no fears
No cries, no tears

A World without crime
Never ending time
Happiness abounds
Joy to be found

A World without strife
Eternal Life
This Life is true
For me, for you

A World coming soon
In night, or noon
It may come in morn
To all be worn

Be ready to go
For this is so
By God's only Son
Our Battles won!!

The Cross that you bear!!

The Cross that you bear
That's upon your shoulders
Feels like a ton
Feels like a boulder

The weight of your Cross
It pulls you down
No longer can you bear
No longer do you care

You've carried your Cross
With a heavy heart to bear
When there is hope
When there is fear

Though your Cross is heavy
God makes your Cross
Feel lighter every way
Feel lighter every day!!

M I P #12

When the storms of life come your way
When all seems lost, all seems hopeless
When despair rears its ugly head
When is now; ask God for help!

The lowest point of your life is right now
The lowest point of your life has hit you hard
The lowest point of your life is at rock bottom
The lowest point of your life; God will lift you up!

Let It Be!!

There are times in our lives
We have complete control
Other times, not one bit

And with these times
That we have no control
We want to have a fit

Not knowing about you
Not knowing at all
But one thing that's for me

It doesn't bother me
Not one single bit
I simply **let it be!!**

There is a Cross!!

There is a Cross that sits on a hill
Its purpose has a special goal
It is a chance of hope for all
To quench your thirsting soul

A man died on this Cross
For us, paid the ultimate cost
Dying for all of our sins
So none of us would be lost

There is a Cross that sits on a hill
It is there for you and for me
To lift your heavy heart up
Come to it on bended knees

If you are weary, worn down
All sorrows to one side toss
Come to a place of blessed peace
Come to Calvary, Come to the Cross!!

Broken wing!!

Is your heart broken?
Like an Eagles Wing
No longer can you fly
No longer can do a thing

Is oh so broken
To the point of despair
Do you really think?
That no one really cares

Is your heart broken?
Pieces on the floor
Your Life's thrown away
Just don't care any more

Take your broken wing
To God, you should give
He will mend it
Giving you a reason to live!!

Loosing Ones' Faith!!

Sometimes we loose our faith
In our fellow man
Sometimes we loose our faith
Of this, I understand

In ourselves, we loose faith
This day has surely come
In ourselves we loose our faith
From this, we can not run

When we loose our faith
Wishing not to live
When we loose our faith
Advice, I freely give

Get down on bended knees
To God, we all should pray
Get down on bended knees
Please to this I dearly say!!

The Light of Sun
The Stars and God!!

Is what to seek when all seems lost?
Is what to seek at any cost?

To delay this, a price you will pay
To delay this, is no other way

It is a leap, by faith of heart
It is a leap, from the very start

The light and sun are close by
The light and sun, give this a try

The stars and God can be found
The stars and God are Heaven bound!!

Giving up the Ghost!!
(pt. 3)

If loosing faith; fast or slow
Don't give in; into woe

There are worries; in your life
There are worries; giving strife

In your life; where you roam
God is there; you're not alone

Don't loose sight; what matters most
Don't give in; in giving up The Ghost!!

Do Not Wish!!

What happened to me
May happen to you
There's no guarantee
No lie, it's true

I went through darkness
Dark as any night
At the time of darkness
There was no light

What I went through
The pain I'd endured
Could you handle it?
To this, are you sure?

What happened to me
No lie, it's true
I wish this on no one
Do not wish this on you!!

Do not wait!!

We think we have plenty of time
To get things right with God
Not realizing how much time
We have here on this sod

All the time in the world
That's what we want to hear
Not carrying about tomorrow
Having no doubts, no fear

If you think you have time
With God to get straight
You are sadly mistaken
For your sake, do not wait!!

Be not you!!

Be not you
To loose faith
Be not you at all

Be not you
To stumble
Be not you to fall

Be not you
To hit a road block
Be not you to hit a wall

When you loose faith
When you stumble
When you fall

When you hit a road block
When you hit it hard
When you hit a wall

Let it be you
To pray to God
To help you through!

Hanging tough!!
(This is me, this is you!!)

It's not over, till it's over
No matter how long it takes

It's not over, till it's over
Until then, I'll hang in there

It's not over, till it's over
Life, give me your best shot

It's not over, till it's over
Until then, I'm hanging tough!!

Printed in the United States
By Bookmasters